THE
BRITISH PHAROS.

Alan Stevenson

THE BRITISH PHAROS;

OR A LIST OF THE

LIGHTHOUSES

ON THE COASTS OF

GREAT BRITAIN AND IRELAND,

DESCRIPTIVE OF THE

APPEARANCE OF THE LIGHTS AT NIGHT.

FOR THE USE OF MARINERS.

SECOND EDITION.

LEITH:
PUBLISHED AND SOLD BY W. REID & SON;
AND TO BE HAD OF ALL THE CHART-SELLERS
IN THE UNITED KINGDOM.

MDCCCXXXI.

ENTERED IN STATIONERS' HALL.

PRINTED BY NEILL & CO., EDINBURGH.

PREFACE

TO THE

FIRST EDITION.

THERE can be no better proof of the utility of Lighthouses on the coast of a country, than the rapid increase of their number wherever the growing trade of that country demands a greater facility and security in the navigation of its shores. Accordingly, we find, in the page of history, that, in the reigns preceding that of ELIZABETH, no exertion was made to improve the maritime state of England, because the limited commerce of the country made few calls for, and gave little encouragement to, any attempts to render the navigation of its shores more safe or easy. But during the reign of that enlightened princess, when more liberal sentiments prevailed in the cabinet of the kingdom, we find, that the masters, wardens, and assistants of the Trinity House, were empowered to erect " beacons, marks, and signs for the sea," wherever they might see such erections to be necessary for the safety of shipping: And, since that time, the labours of this Board expanding with the increasing importance of the commerce of England, and providing for the safety of her navigators, no less than eighty Lighthouses, including Harbour Lights, have been placed along her shores.

The coast of Scotland also was long without the benefit of public lights. In the year 1786, when the Commissioners of Northern Lighthouses were erected into a Board, the only lights upon the Scottish coast were under private or local trusts; and were those of the Isle of May, in the Frith of Forth, Buttonness, in the Frith of Tay, and Cumbrae, in the Frith of Clyde. Since that period, their number, including Harbour Lights, has been increased to about fifty.

The political misfortunes of Ireland were long very injurious to its best interests, and deferred to a later date the time of its maritime improvement. It was not until the year 1810, that the Corporation for preserving and improving the Port of Dublin was established by Act of Parliament, with power to erect Lighthouses on the coast of that country. Before that time, the Lighthouses in Ireland were few in number; but through the praiseworthy exertions of this corporation, upwards of thirty Lighthouses have already been erected on that coast.

The Lights upon the shores of Great Britain and Ireland are now so numerous, and additional ones are still so much called for by the mariner, that the difficulty of knowing one light from another is daily increasing; while the means of varying them are very circumscribed. It is consequently of much importance to have an accurate description of the nightly appearance of each Light, by reference to which, the mariner may be able readily to recognise them, and thus to become aware of the part of the coast off which he may be. The numerous books of charts and sailing directions are minute in their details as to the bearings of the several headlands and dangers of the coast; but there still seems to be wanting a brief account of the Lights (in the order in which they occur on the coast), descriptive of the appearance of each of them at night.

To supply this defect, has been my object in compiling the following pages. In doing this, I have had some advantages, in having navigated, with little exception, the whole coast of the United Kingdom; and also in having had access to some manuscript Notes made by my Father on this subject, in the course of his frequent professional visits to those shores, during a period of nearly thirty years.

I may also add, that I have recently navigated the shores of the Continent, from St Petersburg to the Garonne; and have likewise collected information with regard to the Lighthouses of the Mediterranean; and that I have in view the extension of this List to these Shores.

ALAN STEVENSON.

CONTENTS.

LIGHTS ON THE ENGLISH COAST.

	Page
Berwick Harbour Light,	1
Fern Lights,	2
Blyth Harbour Lights,	3
Tynemouth Castle Light,	ib.
River Tyne Harbour Lights,	4
Sunderland Harbour Lights,	ib.
Whitby Harbour Light,	5
Scarborough Harbour Light,	6
Flamborough Head Light,	ib.
Spurn Lights,	7
Spurn Floating-Light Vessel,	8
Dudgeon Floating-Light Vessel,	9
Lynn Well Floating-Light Vessel,	ib.
Lynn Regis Harbour Light,	10
Hunstanton Light,	ib.
Cromer Light,	11
Hasborough Lights,	ib.

CONTENTS.

	Page
Wintertonness Lights,	12
Winterton Light,	13
Newarp Floating-Light Vessel,	ib.
Stanford Floating-Light Vessel,	14
Leostoffe Lights,	15
Heligoland Light,	ib.
Orfordness Lights,	16
Gallopper Floating-Light Vessel,	17
Sunk Floating-Light Vessel,	18
Harwich Lights,	ib.
Nore Floating-Light Vessel,	19
Margate Harbour Lights,	20
North Foreland Light,	21
Ramsgate Harbour Light,	ib.
Goodwin Floating-Light Vessel,	22
Gull Stream Floating-Light Vessel,	23
South Foreland Lights,	ib.
Dover Harbour Lights,	24
Calais Harbour Lights,	25
Folkestone Harbour Light,	26
Dungeness Light,	ib.
Rye Harbour Lights,	ib.
Beachy Head Light,	27
Newhaven Harbour Lights,	ib.
Brighton Chain-Pier Light,	28
Storeham Harbour Lights,	ib.
Owers Floating-Light Vessel,	29
Bembridge Floating-Light Vessel,	30
Hurst Castle Lights,	31

CONTENTS.

	Page
Needles Light,	32
Portland Lights,	ib.
Casket Lights,	33
Eddystone Light,	34
Plymouth Breakwater Floating-Light Vessel,	ib.
Plymouth Harbour Light,	35
Lizard Lights,	36
Longships Light,	37
St Agnes Light,	ib.
Lundy Island Lights,	38
Bideford Harbour Lights,	ib.
Ilfracombe Harbour Light,	39
Burnham or Bridgewater Harbour Light,	40
Flatholm Light,	ib.
Usk Light,	41
Swansea Harbour Light,	ib.
Mumbles Light,	42
Pembrey Harbour Light,	ib.
St Anne's Lights,	43
Small's Light,	ib.
Aberystwith Harbour Lights,	44
Bradsea Light,	ib.
South Stack Light,	45
Holyhead Harbour Lights,	46
Skerries Light,	ib.
Amlwich Harbour Lights,	47
Linis Point Light,	ib.
Point of Ayre Light in Flintshire,	48
Liverpool Floating-Light Vessel,	ib.

CONTENTS.

	Page
Hoyle Lake Lights,	49
Bidstonhill and Lizza or Leasowe Lights,	ib.
Black Rock Light,	50
Liverpool Dock Lights,	ib.
Liverpool Ferry Lights,	51
Lytham Harbour Light,	ib.
Walney Light,	52
Lancaster Harbour Light,	ib.
Ulverstone Harbour Light,	ib.
St Bees Head Light,	53
Whitehaven Harbour Lights,	ib.
Harrington Harbour Light,	54
Workington Harbour Lights,	ib.
Maryport Harbour Light,	ib.

LIGHTS ON THE ISLE OF MAN.

Point of Ayre Light,	57
Ramsey Harbour Light,	58
Douglas Harbour Light,	ib.
Derby Haven Harbour Light,	ib.
Castletown Harbour Light,	59
Port Le Marie Light,	ib.
Calf of Man Lights,	60
Peel Harbour Light,	ib.

LIGHTS ON THE SCOTTISH COAST.

	Page
Saterness Light,	65
Mull of Galloway Light,	66
Portpatrick Harbour Light,	ib.
Corsewall Light,	67
Ayr Harbour Lights,	ib.
Troon Harbour Light,	68
Ardrossan Harbour Light,	69
Cumbrae Light,	ib.
Toward Light,	70
Clough Light,	ib.
Greenock Harbour Light,	71
Port-Glasgow Harbour Light,	ib.
Bowling Bay Harbour Light,	72
Glasgow or Broomielaw Quay Light,	ib.
Pladda Lights,	73
Campbelton Harbour Light,	ib.
Mull of Kintyre Light,	74
Rhinns of Islay Light,	ib.
Lismore Light,	75
Bara Head Light,	76
Island Glass Light,	ib.
Stornoway Harbour, in the Lewis Isles,	77
Cape Wrath Light,	ib.
Dunnet Head Light,	78
Sumburgh Head Light,	ib.

CONTENTS.

	Page
Start Point Light,	79
Pentland Skerries Lights,	80
Tarbetness Light,	81
Kinnaird Head Light,	ib.
Buchanness Light,	82
Aberdeen Harbour Light,	ib.
Girdleness,	83
Montrose Harbour Lights,	ib.
Arbroath Harbour Light,	84
Bell Rock Light,	ib.
Buttonness Lights,	85
South Ferry Ness Lights,	86
Dundee Harbour Lights,	87
Dundee Ferry Lights,	ib.
Isle of May Light,	88
Carr Rock Beacon,	ib.
Inchkeith Light,	89
Leith Harbour Light,	90
Newhaven Harbour Light,	91
Kinghorn Harbour Light,	ib.
Burntisland Harbour Light,	92
Queensferry Lights,	ib.

LIGHTS ON THE IRISH COAST.

	Page
Dublin Harbour Light,	97
Kingstown Harbour Light,	98
Howth Bayley Light,	ib.
Howth Harbour Light,	99
Kish Bank Floating-Light Vessel,	ib.
Wicklow Head Lights,	100
Arklow Bank Floating Light Vessel,	ib.
Tusker Light,	101
Saltees Coningbeg Floating-Light Vessel,	102
Hook Tower Light,	103
Dunmore Harbour Light,	103
Duncannon Lights,	104
Cork Light,	ib.
Kinsale Harbour Light,	105
Old Head of Kinsale Light,	ib.
Cape Clear Light,	106
Skelligs Rock Lights,	ib.
Loophead Light,	107
Kilkadraan Head Light,	108
South Arran Light,	ib.
Galway Harbour Light,	109
Sline Head Dight,	ib.
Clare Island Light,	110
Westport and Newport Harbour Light,	ib.
Eagle Island Light,	111

CONTENTS.

	Page
Killybegs Light,	ib.
Arran More, or North Arran Light,	112
Tory Island Light,	ib.
Loughswilly Light,	113
Innistrahull Light,	ib.
Maiden or Hulin Rocks Lights,	114
Copeland Light,	ib.
Donaghadee Harbour Light,	115
South Rock Light,	ib.
Ardglass Harbour Light,	116
Carlingford Lights,	ib.
Carlingford Lough Light,	117
Balbriggan Harbour Light,	ib.

LIGHTS

ON THE

ENGLISH COAST.

BERWICK HARBOUR LIGHT.

This light is erected on the pier-head, and starboard hand in entering the harbour of Berwick-upon-Tweed. Here two *stationary* lights are exhibited from the same tower, the one higher than the other. The higher light has a natural or starlike appearance, and is lighted throughout the night; but the lower light, which is of a brilliant red colour, is only shewn while there are 10 feet water upon the bar. The red light will be seen at the distance of one or two leagues, and the other at the distance of two or three leagues, according to the state or clearness of the atmosphere.

FERN LIGHTS.

Situate on the Fern Islands, lying off Bamborough Castle, in the county of Northumberland.

Two of the Fern Lights *revolve*, and one is *stationary*. The *revolving* lights are erected, the higher one upon the main or Fern Island, and the lower upon the Longstone, bearing from each other W. S. W., and E. N. E., and are leading lights for the Navistone. They appear once in every minute, like two stars of the first magnitude, at the distance of four or five leagues, according to the clearness or state of the atmosphere. After attaining their brightest state, these lights gradually become less luminous, and at length are eclipsed.

The *stationary* light is also erected upon the main or Fern Island, and when seen in one and the same direction with the higher *revolving* light, above noticed, leads directly over the Megstone Rock. These two are also leading lights for the Goldstone Rock, and other foul ground in a north-western direction from the Megstone.

BLYTH HARBOUR LIGHTS.

THESE lights are erected on the larboard hand, in entering the river Blyth in the county of Northumberland. Here two *stationary* lights are exhibited, while there is a depth of 8 feet water upon the bar. They bear N. N. W. and S. S. E. from each other, and are visible at the distance of one or two leagues, according to the state of the atmosphere. During the same period of tide in the day, a flag is hoisted.

TYNEMOUTH CASTLE LIGHT.

Situate on the northern side of the entrance to the River Tyne, in the county of Northumberland.

HERE the light *revolves*, and is seen at the distance of five or six leagues, and at less distances in an obscure state of the atmosphere. The light appears, in its brightest state, once in every minute, like a star of the first magnitude; but, gradually becoming less luminous, it is at length eclipsed.

RIVER TYNE HARBOUR LIGHTS

Are situate within the river, at the town of North Shields, in the county of Northumberland. These lights are *stationary*, placed on the starboard hand in entering the river, and are shewn from separate towers, the one higher than the other. They form a leading direction in entering the Tyne, and are seen like two stars of the first magnitude, at the distance of one or two leagues, and at less distances in a cloudy state of the atmosphere. There are about 7 feet water upon the bar at low water of spring tides; and the lights are exhibited from the first quarter of flood, to the first quarter of ebb. During the same period of tide in the day, a flag is hoisted.

SUNDERLAND HARBOUR LIGHTS

Are placed on each side of the entrance of the river Weir, in the county of Durham. These two lights are *stationary*, the one higher than the other. The light upon the northern pier, which is the higher, is exhibited throughout the night, and is seen like a star of the first magnitude, at the distance of three or four leagues, and at less distances in a hazy state of the atmosphere. The lower light, upon the southern pier, is lighted when the wind and tide are favourable for entering the harbour, from about half flood till the first quarter of ebb, and will be seen at the distance of one or two leagues. During the same period of tide, in the day, a flag is hoisted.

WHITBY HARBOUR LIGHT

Is erected on the Western Pier, on the starboard hand, in entering Whitby Harbour, in the county of York. This light is *stationary*, and is seen at the distance of one or two leagues, according to the state of the atmosphere. It is exhibited while there are 8 feet water upon the bar. During same period of the tide, in the day, a flag is hoisted on the West Cliff.

SCARBOROUGH HARBOUR LIGHT

Is erected on the starboard hand, in entering the Harbour of Scarborough, in Yorkshire. It is *stationary*, and is seen at the distance of one or two leagues, and at less distances when the sky is overcast. It is lighted while there are 12 feet water at the entrance. During the same period of tide, in the day, a flag is hoisted.

FLAMBOROUGH HEAD LIGHT.

Placed on the eastern Headland of that name in Yorkshire.

This light *revolves*, exhibiting from the same light-room two lights, like stars of the first magnitude, the one after the other, and then a light of a brilliant red colour; each of these three appearing at intervals of two minutes. After being at their brightest state, they gradually become less luminous, and are eclipsed. The lights of the natural or star-like appearance are visible at the distance of six leagues, and the red light at three or four leagues, and at less distances in a misty state of the atmosphere.

SPURN LIGHTS.

Situate upon a peninsular piece of ground on the starboard or northern side of the entrance to the river Humber in Yorkshire.

THE Spurn Lights are *stationary*, and erected upon separate towers. They exhibit two lights, the one higher than the other, which appear like stars of the first magnitude, at the distance of three or four leagues, and at less distances, according to the state of the atmosphere. When seen in one line, they bear from each other N. W. ½ N., and S. E. ½ S. When the low light is open to the eastward of the high light, it is proper, in steering into the Humber, to haul up till the Floating-light in the offing bears E., and the high light N. N. E.

Note.—*Owing to the continued and recently rapid encroachments of the Sea, it has been resolved in the mean time to discontinue the use of the Lower Lighthouse, and to supply its place by the exhibition of a Temporary Light in the same line of bearing from the Higher Light.*

SPURN FLOATING-LIGHT VESSEL.

Moored in 9 fathoms water, about one league S. E. by E. ½ E. from the Spurn Lights on the coast of Yorkshire.

The Spurn Float exhibits one light, which appears *steady*, or in *motion*, according to the state of the weather. It is visible at the distance of two or three leagues, and at different distances, in relation to the clearness or haziness of the atmosphere. In the day, a flag is displayed from the mast-head; and during foggy weather and snow-showers a bell is tolled night and day.

DUDGEON FLOATING-LIGHT VESSEL.

Moored in 8 fathoms water, on the south-western side of the Dudgeon Shoal, lying seven leagues N. E. ½ E. from Wells in Norfolk.

The Dudgeon Float exhibits one light, which appears *steady* or *in motion*, according to the state of the weather. It is visible at the distance of two or three leagues, and at other distances relatively to the mistiness or clearness of the atmosphere. In the day, a flag is hoisted at the mast-head; and during foggy weather and snow-showers, a bell is tolled night and day.

LYNN WELL FLOATING-LIGHT VESSEL.

Moored in 22½ fathoms water, off the Hook of Longsand, distant half a mile S. E. from the Buoy on that Sand, and from Hunstanton Light in Norfolk one league N. ½ W.

The Lynn Well Float exhibits two lights of the same height upon separate masts, which appear *steady* or *in motion*, according to the state of the weather. These lights are visible at the distance of two or three leagues, in relation to the state of haziness or clearness of the atmosphere. In the day a flag is hoisted at the mast-head; and during foggy weather and snow-showers, a bell is tolled night and day.

LYNN REGIS HARBOUR LIGHT

Is erected on the Pilot-House of Lynn in Norfolk. This light is *stationary,* and is exhibited by the pilots at the proper time of tide for vessels entering or leaving the harbour.

HUNSTANTON LIGHT.

Situate on the coast of Norfolk, about five leagues N. E. of Lynn.

This light is *stationary*, appearing like a star of the first magnitude, at the distance of three or four leagues, according to the state of the atmosphere.

CROMER LIGHT.

Situate on one of the north-eastern headland S. of the coast of Norfolk.

This light *revolves,* and is seen at the distance of five or six leagues, according to the state of the atmosphere. The light appears once in every minute, in its brightest state, like a star of the first magnitude; but gradually becoming less luminous, is eclipsed.

HASBOROUGH LIGHTS.

Situate on the eastern coast of Norfolk, between the lights of Cromer and Winterton.

These two light are *stationary,* and are erected upon separate towers, the one higher than the other. They appear like stars of the first magnitude at the distance of three or four leagues, according to the clearness of the atmosphere. When seen in one line, they bear N.

W. ¼ W. and S. E. ¼ E. from each other, and are leading lights through Hasborough Gut, between the Newarp and Ridge Sands.

WINTERTONNESS LIGHTS.

Situate on the coast of Norfolk, 7 miles south-eastward of Hasborough Lights.

THE Wintertonness lights are *stationary*, and erected upon separate towers. They exhibit two lights, the one higher than the other, which appear like stars of the first magnitude, at the distance of three or four leagues, according to the state of the atmosphere. When seen in one line, they bear from each other W. N. W. and E. S. E. They form leading lights for Hasborough Gut.

WINTERTON LIGHT.

Situate on the coast of Norfolk, 7 miles northward of Yarmouth.

This light is *stationary*, appearing like a star of the first magnitude, at the distance of three or four leagues in clear weather. It is useful as a direction for the Cockle Gut and northern entrance to Yarmouth Roads.

NEWARP FLOATING-LIGHT VESSEL.

Moored in 12 fathoms water at the northern extremity of the Newarp Sand Bank, bearing E. S. E. ½ E. from Winterton Light, distant 6 miles.

Newarp Float exhibits three lights upon separate masts; and the main being the highest, the light forms a triangular figure. It is *steady*, or *in motion*, according to the state of the weather, and is visible at the distance of two or three leagues, relatively to the state or clearness of the atmosphere. In the day, a flag is hoisted at the mast-head; and during foggy weather and snow-showers, a bell is tolled night and day.

STANFORD FLOATING-LIGHT VESSEL.

Moored in 4½ fathoms water, bearing S. E. ¾ S. from Leostoffe High Light in Suffolkshire, distant 1 mile.

STANFORD FLOAT exhibits two lights upon a yard *athwart ships* which appear *steady* or *in motion*, according to the state of the weather. The lights are visible at the distance of two or three leagues, according to the clearness of the atmosphere. They serve as a direction for the Stanford Channel. In the day, a flag is hoisted at the mast-head; and during foggy weather and snow-showers, a bell is tolled night and day.

LEOSTOFFE LIGHTS.

Situate at the town of Leostoffe, and eastern point of the county of Suffolk.

THESE lights are *stationary*, and are erected upon separate towers, the one higher than the other. They appear like two stars of the first magnitude, at the distance of three or four leagues, according to the state or clearness of the atmosphere. They bear N. and S. from each other, and, when seen in one line, serve as a leading direction for sailing between the Holme and Newcombe Banks. The high light should be kept open to the west, and brought to bear N. by E.

HELIGOLAND LIGHT.

Erected on the highest part of the Island of Heligoland, situate in North Lat. 54° 11', and East Long. 7° 53', bearing by compass from Leostoffe Light E., distant 81 leagues, and from Cuxhaven N. W. by N., distant 11 leagues.

HELIGOLAND LIGHT is *stationary*, appearing like a star of the first magnitude, at the distance of six or seven leagues, according to the state of the atmosphere.

Note.—This Light was altered from a coal to an oil light, with reflectors, by the British Government during the continental war, about the year 1808, and is therefore noticed here.

ORFORDNESS LIGHTS.

Situate on a projecting point of land eastward from the town of Orford in Suffolkshire.

ORFORDNESS LIGHTS are *stationary*, erected upon separate towers, and exhibit two lights, the one higher than the other. They appear like two stars of the first magnitude, at the distance of three or four leagues, according to the state or clearness of the atmosphere. When seen in one line, they bear from each other S. W. by W. ¼ W. and N. E. by E. ¼ E., and form a leading direction to the north entrance of the Channel, between Aldborough Knapes

Bank and the shore; and also for the south entrance between the Ridge and the Knoll Banks.

GALLOPER FLOATING-LIGHT VESSEL.

Moored in 15 fathoms water, 2 miles south-west of the shoalest part of the Galloper Sand Bank, and 7 leagues S. ½ E. from Orfordness, in the county of Suffolk.

The Galloper Float exhibits two lights from separate masts, which appear *steady* or *in motion*, according to the state of the weather, and are visible at the distance of two or three leagues, according to the state of the atmosphere. In the day, a flag is hoisted at the mast-head; and during foggy weather and snow-showers, a bell is tolled night and day.

SUNK FLOATING-LIGHT VESSEL.

Moored in 8 fathoms water, at the eastern extremity of the Sunk Sandbank, 13 miles S. by E. ¼ E. from Harwich Lights, in the county of Essex.

The Sunk Float exhibits one light, which appears *steady* or *in motion*, according to the state of the weather. The light is visible at the distance of two or three leagues, according to the state of cloudiness or clearness of the atmosphere. In the day, a flag is hoisted at the mast-head; and during foggy weather and snow-showers, a bell is tolled night and day. At intervals of every half hour, the bell is struck six times in ten minutes, to distinguish it from other Floating-lights. This light is a chief direction for the Sunk and King's Channels leading to the Thames.

HARWICH LIGHTS.

Situate at the town of Harwich, in the county of Essex.

These two lights are *stationary*, and erected upon separate towers, the one somewhat higher than the other. They appear like stars of the first magnitude, at the distance of three or four leagues, according to the state of the atmosphere. When seen in one line, they bear from each other N. N. W. ½ W. and S. S. E. ½ E. and are leading lights over the Rolling Ground, and for the Church and other sand-banks in the track to Harwich and Ipswich. The landward tower is carried 40 feet above the light-room, and is useful as a sea-mark by day.

NORE FLOATING-LIGHT VESSEL.

Moored in 4 fathoms water, about three miles E. N. E. ¾ E. from Garrison Point, at Sheerness, in Kent.

THE Nore Float exhibits one light, which appears *steady* or *in motion*, according to the state of the weather. It is visible at the distance of two or three leagues, according to the state of dulness or clearness of the atmosphere. In the day, a flag is hoisted at the mast-head; and during foggy weather and snow-showers, a bell is tolled night and day. This light is a direction for the Thames and entrance of the Medway.

MARGATE HARBOUR LIGHTS

ARE erected, the one on the Pier-head, the other on the Jetty; and both are taken on the larboard hand in entering the Harbour of Margate, in the county of Kent. These two lights are *stationary*. That upon the Pier-head is of a natural or star-like appearance, and is seen at the distance of one or two leagues, according to the state or clearness of the atmosphere. The light upon the Jetty, which extends in a northerly direction from the east end of the pier, is of a red colour, and is seen at the distance of about one league. These lights are exhibited while there are 10 feet water in the harbour; and during the same period of tide in the day a flag is hoisted.

NORTH FORELAND LIGHT.

Erected upon the most northern Headland of the county of Kent.

THE North Foreland Light is *stationary*, appearing like a star of the first magnitude, at the distance of six or seven leagues, according to the state or clearness of the atmosphere.

RAMSGATE HARBOUR LIGHT

Is erected on the South Pier and larboard hand, in entering the harbour of Ramsgate, in the county of Kent. This light is *stationary*, and is seen at the distance of two or three leagues, according to the state of the atmosphere. It is exhibited while there are 10 feet water between the pier-heads; and in the day a flag is hoisted on the cliff near Jacob's Ladder, while there is the same depth of water in the harbour.

Note.—It is estimated, that, in about an

hour after the 10 feet signal is made, the depth of water increases to 16 feet—in about two hours to 20 feet—and in three hours after, or about high water, to 21 feet. In neap-tides as above, there are the varying depths of 14, 17, and 18 feet between the pier-heads.

GOODWIN FLOATING-LIGHT VESSEL.

Moored in 9 fathoms water, about ¾ mile E. ½ S. from the North Sand Head of the Goodwin, and 7 miles S. S. E. ½ E. from the North Foreland Light, in the county of Kent.

THE Goodwin Float exhibits three lights upon separate masts, which, from the mainmast being the highest, have a triangular figure. These lights appear *steady* or *in motion*, according to the state of the weather; and are visible at the distance of two or three leagues, relatively to the state of clearness or obscurity of the atmosphere. In the day a flag is hoisted at the mast head; and during foggy weather and snow-showers, a bell is tolled night and day.

GULL STREAM FLOATING-LIGHT VESSEL

Is moored in 8 fathoms water off Trinity Swash, one of the tracks connected with the anchorage of the Downs; and bears N. E. by E., distant 9 miles from the South Foreland Lights, in the county of Kent.

The Gull Stream Float exhibits upon a yard *athwart ships*, two lights, which appear *steady* or *in motion* according to the state of the weather. The lights are visible at the distance of two or three leagues, relatively to the state of the atmosphere. In the day a flag is hoisted at the mast-head; and during foggy weather and snow-showers, a bell is tolled night and day.

SOUTH FORELAND LIGHTS.

Situate between Deal and Dover in the county of Kent.

These two lights are *stationary*, erected upon separate towers, the one higher than the other, and appear like two stars of the first magnitude, at the distance of five or six leagues, according to the state of the atmosphere. When seen in one line, they bear from each other W. by N. and E. by S., and are leading lights for the Goodwin Sands.

DOVER HARBOUR LIGHTS.

ARE elevated upon masts on the Southern Pier or larboard hand in entering the Harbour of Dover, in the county of Kent. These two lights are *stationary*, appearing like stars, the one higher than the other, at the distance of two or three leagues, according to the state of the atmosphere. When seen in one line, they bear from each other N. N. W. and S. S. E., and form a leading direction into the harbour of Dover, while there is a depth of 10 feet water. In the day, a flag is hoisted while there is the same depth of water in the harbour.

CALAIS HARBOUR LIGHTS

Situate at Calais, in the *Department du Pas du Calais*. These two lights are erected upon separate towers, on the starboard hand in entering the harbour. They bear from each other S. ¼ E. and N. ½ W. The light upon Fort Rouge, at the immediate entrance, is *stationary*, but that which is more landward *revolves*, and is seen in its brightest state once in every three minutes, but gradually becoming less luminous, is eclipsed. Both lights are of the natural or star-like appearance, and will be seen at the distance of four or five leagues, according to the state of clearness or obscurity of the atmosphere.

These lights are exhibited while there is a depth of 10 feet water in the harbour. In the day, a flag is hoisted during the same period of tide.

Note.—These Lights belong to the French Government, but are noticed here from their proximity to the English coast.

FOLKESTONE HARBOUR LIGHT

Is situate on the larboard hand in entering the harbour of Folkestone, in the county of Kent. This light is exhibited while there are 9 feet water in the harbour, and has a star-like appearance, at the distance of one or two leagues, according to the state of clearness or haziness of the atmosphere.

DUNGENESS LIGHT.

Situate in the county of Kent, upon a projecting point of land between Dover and Beachy Head.

This light is *stationary*, appearing like a star of the first magnitude, at the distance of four or five leagues, according to the state of the atmosphere. To distinguish it as a sea-mark in the day, the lighthouse tower is painted *red*.

RYE HARBOUR LIGHTS

Are erected upon the starboard hand in entering the harbour of Rye, in the county of

Sussex. These lights are *stationary*, appearing like two stars, the one higher than the other. They are exhibited while there is a depth of 9 feet water on the bar. In the day a flag is hoisted, while there is the same depth of water upon the bar.

BEACHY HEAD LIGHT.

Situate on the Headland of that name in the county of Sussex.

This light *revolves*, and will be seen at the distance of six or seven leagues, according to the clearness of the atmosphere. It appears once in every two minutes in its brightest state, like a star of the first magnitude, and gradually becoming less luminous, is eclipsed.

NEWHAVEN HARBOUR LIGHTS

Are situate on the larboard hand in entering the harbour of Newhaven, in the county of

Sussex. These two lights are exhibited throughout the night, from September to May inclusive. They have a star-like appearance at the distance of one or two leagues, according to the state of the atmosphere.

BRIGHTON CHAIN-PIER LIGHT.

A SMALL LIGHT is exhibited at the outer extremity of the Chain-Pier of Brightelmstone or Brighton. It is lighted throughout the night, chiefly for the use of the steam-boats. The light is of a *bluish* colour, and is seen at the distance of one or two leagues, according to the state of clearness or obscurity of the atmosphere.

STOREHAM HARBOUR LIGHTS

ARE situate at the entrance of the harbour of Shoreham, in the county of Sussex. These lights appear like two stars, the one higher than the other. The higher one is exhibited throughout the night, and the lower one is lighted while it is the proper time for vessels to enter the harbour. They are visible at the distance of one or two leagues, according to the state of the atmosphere.

OWERS FLOATING-LIGHT VESSEL.

Moored in 7 fathoms water, six miles S. S. E. ½ E. from Selsea Bill, in the county of Sussex.

THE Owers Float exhibits one light, which appears *steady* or *in motion*, according to the state of the weather. The light is visible at the distance of two or three leagues, relatively to the state of clearness or dulness of the atmosphere. In the day a flag is displayed from the mast-head; and during foggy weather and snow-showers, a bell is tolled night and day.

Note.—The signal made from the floating light stationed off the *Owers Rocks* to warn vessels of their danger when approaching those shoals in an improper direction, having not been at all times perceived or understood; the Trinity Board have given notice, that so soon as a vessel shall be seen by the crew of the Light-vessel in a dangerous course towards these rocks, a *gun will be fired* on board the Light-vessel, and immediately thereafter a red flag at the mast-head will *be lowered half-mast,* and so continued until the vessel in danger shall have altered her course.

BEMBRIDGE FLOATING-LIGHT VESSEL.

Moored in 5 fathoms water, about 140 *fathoms east from the Buoy of the Nab Rock, lying* 2¼ *miles S. E. by E. from Great St Helens, in the Isle of Wight.*

The Bembridge Float exhibits two lights upon separate masts, the one higher than the other, which appear *steady* or *in motion,* according to the state of the weather. These lights are visible at the distance of two or three leagues, relatively to the state of clearness or obscurity of the atmosphere. In the day a flag is hoisted at the mast-head; and during foggy weather and snow-showers, a bell is tolled night and day.

HURST CASTLE LIGHTS.

Situate upon the beach at Hurst Castle, on the northern side of the Needles Passage in Hampshire.

HURST LIGHTS are *stationary*, and are erected upon separate towers. They exhibit two lights, the one higher than the other, appearing like stars of the first magnitude, at the distance of three or four leagues, according to the state of the atmosphere. When seen in one line, they bear from each other N. E. by E. ½ E. and S. W. by W. ½ W., and are leading lights for the Needles Bridge and Shingles.

NEEDLES LIGHT.

Situate upon the western headland of the Isle of Wight in Hampshire.

The Needles Light is *stationary*, appearing like a star of the first magnitude, at the distance of five or six leagues, according to the state of the atmosphere.

PORTLAND LIGHTS.

Situate upon the Bill or southern extremity of the peninsula called Portland Island, in Dorsetshire.

The Portland Lights are erected upon separate towers, the one higher than the other. The lower light is *stationary*; but the higher light *revolves*, and is seen in full force once in every two minutes. Both lights, when in view, appear like stars of the first magnitude, at the distance of five and six leagues respectively, according to the clear or cloudy state of the atmosphere. When seen in one line, they bear from each other N.N.W. ¼ W. and S.S.E. ½ E. and are leading lights for Portland Race and the Shambles.

Note.—Till the year 1824, both lights at Portland were *stationary*.

CASKET LIGHTS,

Erected upon the Casket Rock or Islet, situate about 6 miles from the north-western point of the island of Alderney.

These lights *revolve*, appearing like three stars of the first magnitude, at the distance of four or five leagues, according to the state of the atmosphere. The lights appear in full strength once in every minute; but gradually becoming less luminous, are eclipsed. They form a triangular figure, excepting when seen upon a south-east bearing, when only two of them are visible.

EDDYSTONE LIGHT.

The Rock on which this Lighthouse is erected, is situate at the entrance of Plymouth Sound, about 9 miles S.W. ¾ S. from the Ramhead in Cornwall.

The Eddystone Light is *stationary*, appearing from all points of the compass like a star of the first magnitude, at the distance of four or five leagues, according to the state of the atmosphere.

Note.—For an account of the building of this celebrated edifice, see " Smeaton's Narrative of the Eddystone Lighthouse."

PLYMOUTH BREAKWATER FLOATING-LIGHT VESSEL.

Moored in 7 fathoms water off the western extremity of the Breakwater, which bears E.N.E. ½ E., distant 1½ miles from Pen-Point, and distant ¾ miles south from Redding Point, in the county of Cornwall.

The Breakwater Float exhibits two lights upon a yard *athwart ships*, which appear *steady* or *in motion,* according to the state of the weather. The lights are seen at the distance of one or two leagues, but at lesser distances when the atmosphere is not clear. In the day a flag is hoisted at the mast-head; and during foggy weather and snow-showers, a bell is toiled night and day.

Note.—This light is understood to be temporary, but will be continued until a lighthouse be erected upon the Breakwater.

PLYMOUTH HARBOUR LIGHT.

SITUATE on the larboard-hand in entering the harbour of Plymouth in Devonshire. This light is *stationary,* and is exhibited throughout the night, having a star-like appearance at the distance of one or two leagues, and at lesser distances in hazy weather. This light is useful as a direction for sailing through the passage to the east of the Breakwater; and when shut in by Fish-Nose, at the eastern extremity of the Citadel, it also serves as a guide for the Cobbler Shoal, off Mount Batten.

LIZARD LIGHTS.

Situate on the Lizard Point, the south-eastern headland of the county of Cornwall.

The Lizard Lights are *stationary*, erected upon separate towers, the one higher than the other, and appearing like two stars of the first magnitude, at the distance of six or seven leagues, according to the state of the atmosphere. When seen in one line, they bear from each other E. and W., and are leading lights in passing the Stags and Manacle Rocks.

LONGSHIPS LIGHT.

Erected upon the highest of the Longships Rocks, situate 3 miles off the south-eastern extremity of the Land's End of Cornwall.

The Longships Light is *stationary*, appearing like a star of the first magnitude, from all points of the compass, at the distance of four or five leagues, according to the state of the atmosphere.

ST AGNES LIGHT.

Erected upon St Agnes, one of the Scilly Islands.

ST AGNES LIGHT *revolves*, and is seen at the distance of five or six leagues, or at lesser distances in a hazy atmosphere. The light appears once in every minute in its brightest state, like a star of the first magnitude, but gradually becoming less luminous, is eclipsed.

LUNDY ISLAND LIGHTS.

Situate on Lundy Island, at the entrance of the Bristol Channel, about 9 miles N. ¼ E. from Hartland Point in Devonshire.

Lundy Lights consist of a *stationary* and a *revolving* light. The latter revolves so rapidly, as hardly to exhibit any interval of darkness, and is seen at all points of the compass; but the stationary light is seen only from N. N. W. to W. S. W., and intervening points westerly. These lights appear like stars of the first magnitude, at the distance of six or seven leagues, or at lesser distances in hazy weather.

BIDEFORD HARBOUR LIGHTS.

Situate on the Devonshire side, at the entrance of the Bristol Channel. These two lights are *stationary*, and are erected upon separate towers, the one higher than the other.

When seen in one line, they bear from each other N. W. ¾ W., and S. E. ¾ E., and are leading lights for crossing the bar to the harbours of Appledale and Barnstaple. The lights are exhibited from half-tide of flood to half-tide of ebb; and in the day a flag is hoisted at the same periods of the tide.

ILFRACOMBE HARBOUR LIGHT

Is placed upon the Devonshire side, within the Bristol Channel, and about 20 miles W. by N. from Lundy Island. This light is *stationary*, and of a starlike appearance. It is exhibited throughout the night during the winter months, or from Michaelmas to Lady Day; and is seen at the distance of one or two leagues, or at lesser distances when the atmosphere is hazy.

BURNHAM OR BRIDGEWATER HARBOUR LIGHT.

Situate on the larboard hand in entering the River Perret, leading to Bridgewater in Somersetshire. This light appears in full force like a star one minute and a half, and is then eclipsed half a minute. It is lighted throughout the night, and is seen at the distance of one or two leagues, according to the state of cloudiness or clearness of the atmosphere.

FLATHOLM LIGHT.

Situate on the island of Flatholm, in the Bristol Channel, 20 leagues E. S. E. ½ E. from Lundy Island lights.

This light is *stationary*, appearing like a star of the first magnitude, at the distance of four or five leagues, according to the state of the atmosphere.

USK LIGHT.

Situate on the larboard side in entering the River Usk, leading to Newport in Monmouthshire.

This light is *stationary*, appearing like a star of the first magnitude, at the distance of two or three leagues, or at lesser distances, when the atmosphere is in an unfavourable state.

SWANSEA HARBOUR LIGHT.

Situate on the larboard pier-head in entering the harbour of Swansea in Glamorganshire. This light is *stationary*, and of a brilliant red colour. It is visible at the distance of one or two leagues, or at lesser distances in hazy weather: It is lighted while there are 8 feet water in the harbour.

Note.—This light had formerly a natural or star-like appearance.

MUMBLES LIGHT.

Situate upon a point of land called the Mumbles, forming the western chop of Swansea Bay, in the county of Glamorgan.

This light is *stationary*, appearing like a star of the first magnitude, at the distance of four or five leagues, or at lesser distances in hazy weather.

PEMBREY HARBOUR LIGHT.

Situate on the larboard hand in entering Burry River, in the county of Caermarthen. This light is *stationary*, and of a star-like appearance. It is lighted while there are 10 feet water in the harbour. To prevent its being mistaken for the Mumbles Light, it is *masked* seaward, and is not visible till vessels pass the Holms, an island at the entrance of the river. In the day a flag is hoisted while there are ten feet of water in the harbour.

CALDY ISLAND LIGHT.

Placed on Caldy island, which forms the western chop of Caermarthen Bay, in the county of Pembroke.

This light is *stationary*, appearing like a star of the first magnitude, at the distance of three or four leagues, and at lesser distances in hazy weather.

ST ANNE'S LIGHTS.

Situate on St Anne's Head, forming the western chop of the entrance to Milford Haven in Pembrokeshire.

These lights are *stationary*, erected upon separate towers, the one higher than the other, and appearing like two stars of the first magnitude, at the distance of four or five leagues, according to the state of the atmosphere. When seen in one line, they bear from each other N. by W. ¼ W., and S. by E. ¼ E., and are leading lights for the Crow Rock, on the starboard side of the entrance to Milford Haven.

SMALL'S LIGHT

Is erected upon the largest of the Small's Rocks, lying off St David's Head in Pembrokeshire, and bearing from St Anne's Lights N. W. by W. distant 18 miles.

The Small's Light is *stationary*, appearing, from all points of the compass, like a star of the first magnitude, at the distance of three or four leagues, according to the state or clearness of the atmosphere.

ABERYSTWITH HARBOUR LIGHTS,

In Cardiganshire, are *stationary*, and form two leading lights for entering this harbour. They are exhibited at the proper time of tide, but only when vessels are expected to enter the harbour.

BRADSEA LIGHT.

Situate on the south-western extremity of Bradsea Island in Caernarvonshire, which is separated from Brach-y-Pwll by a channel of about 3 miles in breadth.

This light may be made known to mariners as a *flashing light*, which, from being feeble, suddenly becomes bright, like a star of the first magnitude. It is visible at the distance of five or six leagues, according to the state of the atmosphere. The lantern is open from E. to N. E. by N., and intervening points of the compass southerly.

SOUTH STACK LIGHT.

Situate on the small island of that name, which is almost contiguous to the Southern extremity of the promontory of Holyhead in Anglesea.

THE South Stack Light *revolves*, and is seen at the distance of six or seven leagues, according to the state of the atmosphere. The light appears once in every two minutes, in its brightest state, like a star of the first magnitude, and gradually becoming less luminous, is eclipsed. The lantern is open from N. E. by E. ¼ E. to S. E., and intervening points of the compass westerly.

HOLYHEAD HARBOUR LIGHTS.

Situate on the starboard hand in entering Holyhead Harbour, in the island of Anglesea. These lights are *stationary*. The higher or principal light appears like a star of the first magnitude, at the distance of three or four leagues, according to the state of the atmosphere; while the lower light, which is of a brilliant red colour, is visible only in a N. N. W. direction, at the distance of about one league, being chiefly useful for directing vessels to clear the Outer Platters and rocks lying off the northern part of Salt Island.

SKERRIES LIGHT.

Situate on Skerries Island, lying about 1½ miles off Carnel's Point, at the north-western extremity of the island of Anglesea.

This light is *stationary*, and appears like a star of the first magnitude, from all points of the compass, at the distance of four or five leagues, according to the state of the atmosphere.

AMLWCH HARBOUR LIGHTS

ARE *stationary*, and have a star-like appearance. The two lights are situate at the entrance of the harbour of Amlwch, on the northern side of the Island of Anglesea, and are useful for vessels frequenting this harbour for the copper-ore.

LINIS POINT LIGHT

Is *stationary*, and has a star-like appearance. It is situate at the entrance of the small port of Elian, at the northern extremity of the Island of Anglesea, and is chiefly useful for the Liverpool pilots who frequent this station.

POINT OF AYRE LIGHT IN FLINTSHIRE.

Situate on the south-western side of the entrance of the River Dee.

This light is *stationary*, and appears like a star of the first magnitude, at the distance of three or four leagues, according to the state of the atmosphere.

LIVERPOOL FLOATING-LIGHT VESSEL.

Moored at the entrance of the Horse Channel, in 7 fathoms water, 7 miles N. W. $\frac{1}{4}$ N. from Lizza or Leasowe Light in Cheshire.

The Liverpool Float exhibits three lights upon separate masts, which, from the mainmast being the highest, have a triangular figure. These lights appear *steady* or *in motion*, according to the state of the weather, and are visible at the distance of two or three leagues, relatively to the state of the atmosphere. In the day a flag is hoisted at the mast-head; and during hazy weather and snow-showers, a bell is tolled night and day.

HOYLE LAKE LIGHTS.

Situate on the north-western side of the entrance of the River Dee in Cheshire.

THESE lights are *stationary*, erected upon separate towers, the one somewhat higher than the other; and appear like stars, at the distance of two or three leagues, according to the state of the atmosphere. When seen in one line, they bear from each other S. by W. ½ W., and N. by E. ½ E., and are leading lights for Hoyle Lake Roads.

BIDSTONHILL AND LIZZA OR LEASOWE LIGHTS.

The one erected upon Bidstonhill, and the other upon the sea-shore, between the rivers Mersey and Dee, in Cheshire.

THESE two lights are *stationary*, and are erected upon towers about 2¼ miles apart, Bidstonhill being the higher. They appear like two stars of the first magnitude, at the distance of four and six leagues respectively, according to the state of the atmosphere. When seen in one line, they bear from each other S.E. and N. W., and are leading lights for the Horse Channel.

BLACK ROCK LIGHT.
Situate on the Cheshire side, at the entrance of the river Mersey.

This light *revolves*, exhibiting from the same light-room two lights of the natural appearance, the one after the other, and then a light of a brilliant red colour; each of these three appearing at intervals of one minute, the whole revolution being completed in three minutes. After being at their brightest state, they gradually become less luminous and are eclipsed. During foggy weather and snow-showers, a bell is tolled night and day.

LIVERPOOL DOCK LIGHTS

Are on the Liverpool or Lancashire side of the Mersey. The Ferry Lights consist of three street or globe lamps, arranged in a triangular figure, erected upon a pole at the entrance of Salthouse Dock. They are lighted at the proper time of tide for vessels entering the Docks.

LIVERPOOL FERRY LIGHTS.

On the Cheshire side of the Mersey, consist of lamps placed at the several piers, for the direction of the Ferry-boats.

LYTHAM HARBOUR LIGHT.

Situate upon the larboard hand within the river Ribble, leading to Preston, in Lancashire.

This light is *stationary*, and has a star-like appearance. It is only lighted during tide-time, when vessels are in the river, or when a signal gun is fired at sun-set by any vessel in the channel.

WALNEY LIGHT.

Situate on the southern extremity of the island of Walney in Lancashire, on the larboard hand at the entrance to the navigation toward the ports of Lancaster and Ulverstone.

This light *revolves*, and is seen at the distance of three or four leagues, or at lesser distances, when the atmosphere is hazy. The light appears once in every five minutes in its brightest state, and gradually becoming less luminous, is eclipsed.

LANCASTER HARBOUR LIGHT

Is placed on the Pier or Breakwater about one mile below Lancaster, and consists of a lamp, which is lighted at tide time, to shew the situation of Hash Bank.

ULVERSTONE HARBOUR LIGHT.

On the Pier-head at Ulverston, a lamp is lighted at tide-time as a direction into the canal.

ST BEES HEAD LIGHT.

Situate on St Bees Head, the most western headland of the coast of Cumberland.

This light is *stationary*, appearing like a star of the first magnitude, at the distance of five or six leagues, or at lesser distances when the atmosphere is hazy.

WHITEHAVEN HARBOUR LIGHTS

Are erected upon the outer and inner Pier-heads, in entering the harbour of Whitehaven, in the county of Cumberland. The outer light is *stationary*, and is lighted while there are 9 feet water between the pier-heads. The inner light *revolves*, and is lighted throughout the night. It is seen at the distance of three or four leagues, or at lesser distances in hazy weather. The light appears in its brightest state about once in forty seconds; and gradually becoming less luminous, is eclipsed. In the day a flag is hoisted on an eminence adjacent to the pier, while there are 9 feet water in the harbour.

HARRINGTON HARBOUR LIGHT

Is about four miles northward of Whitehaven. A lantern is hoisted upon a pole on the starboard hand in entering the harbour, while there is a depth of 8 feet water in it.

WORKINGTON HARBOUR LIGHTS

ARE situate on the starboard hand in entering the harbour of Workington in Cumberland, on the southern side of the Solway Frith. These lights have a star-like appearance, and are exhibited while there are 8 feet water in the harbour. They form leading lights for entering it; but at sea only one of the lights is visible.

MARYPORT HARBOUR LIGHT.

SITUATE on the Cumberland side of the Solway Frith, and on the starboard hand in entering the harbour of Maryport. It has a star-like appearance, and is lighted while there are 8 feet water in the harbour.

NOTE.

The Public Lights, and also the Floating Buoys and Beacons on the Coast of England, are under the direction of The Corporation of the Trinity House of London.

LIGHTS

ON THE

ISLE OF MAN.

POINT OF AYRE LIGHT.

Situate on the northern extremity of the Isle of Man.

THIS light *revolves*, exhibiting from the same light-room two lights, the one resembling a star of the first magnitude, and the other being of a brilliant red colour. Each light appears in its brightest state, at intervals of two minutes, and gradually becoming less luminous, is eclipsed. The light of the natural or star-like appearance is visible at the distance of five leagues, and the red light at four leagues, in clear weather; but when the atmosphere is hazy, the lights are not seen at such distances.

RAMSEY HARBOUR LIGHT.

ERECTED on the Pier on the larboaad hand in entering the harbour of Ramsey, is a small *stationary* light of a star-like appearance, exhibited throughout the night, which is visible at the distance of two or three leagues in clear weather.

DOUGLAS HARBOUR LIGHT.

SITUATE at the Pier-head on the starboard hand in entering the harbour of Douglas. The light is *stationary*, and is seen at the distance of two or three leagues, or at lesser distances when the atmosphere is hazy.

DERBY HAVEN HARBOUR LIGHT.

A SMALL *stationary* light of a star-like appearance, at the entrance of Derby Haven. It is exhibited throughout the night during the *season of the herring-fishery*, and is visible at the distance of one or two leagues, or at lesser distances if the atmosphere be hazy.

CASTLETOWN HARBOUR LIGHT.

Placed on the larboard hand in entering the Harbour of Castletown. It is lighted throughout the night during the *season of the herring-fishery;* and, at other times, only when vessels are expected to enter. The light is *stationary* and of a star-like appearance; and is seen at the distance of one or two leagues in clear weather, and at lesser distances when the weather is hazy.

PORT LE MARIE LIGHT.

Placed on the larboard hand in entering Port Le Marie. The light is *stationary*, is lighted throughout the night, and is seen at the distance of one or two leagues, or at lesser distances in hazy weather.

CALF OF MAN LIGHTS.

Situate on the south-western side of the island of Calf of Man, which is separated from the main island of Man by a narrow channel.

CALF OF MAN lights *revolve*, and are placed on separate towers, the one higher than the other. These two lights appear every two minutes, like stars of the first magnitude, and gradually becoming less luminous, are eclipsed. They are seen at the distance of six or seven leagues, according to the state of the atmosphere. When seen in one line, they bear from each other N. E. $\frac{1}{3}$ E. and S. W. $\frac{1}{3}$ W.; and in that position shew the mariner that he is off the sunken rocks called the *Chickens*. The lights are hid by Peel Head toward the east, and by Spanish Head toward the south-east; but both lights are visible at a quarter of a mile off the dangerous point of Langness.

PEEL HARBOUR LIGHT.

PLACED on the larboard hand in entering the harbour of Peel. It is a *stationary* light of a star-like appearance, and is lighted throughout the night. It is seen at the distance of one or two leagues, or at lesser distances if the atmosphere be hazy.

NOTE.

The three Public Lights situate at the Point of Ayre and Calf of Man, belong to the Scotch Lighthouse Board, established at Edinburgh. But the Harbour Lights are under the direction of a Parliamentary Commission, of which the Receiver-General of His Majesty's Customs, Isle of Man, is the Chairman.

LIGHTS

ON THE

SCOTTISH COAST.

LIGHTS

ON THE

SCOTTISH COAST.

SATERNESS LIGHT.

SITUATE on the western side of the Solway Frith, in the Stewartry of Kirkcudbright. The light is *stationary*, and of the natural appearance, and is visible at the distance of two or three leagues, or at lesser distances, according to the state of the atmosphere. It is chiefly useful as a direction to the harbour of Dumfries.

MULL OF GALLOWAY LIGHT.

Erected on the south-eastern extremity of the Mull of Galloway, in Wigtonshire.

THIS light is known to mariners as an *Intermittent Light*, suddenly appearing like a star of the first magnitude, and continuing in view two minutes and a-half; it is then suddenly eclipsed for half a minute, and thus produces its entire effect once in every three minutes. It is visible at the distance of seven or eight leagues, and at lesser distances according to the state of the atmosphere.

PORTPATRICK HARBOUR LIGHT.

SITUATE on the starboard hand in entering the harbour of Portpatrick in Wigtonshire. This light is *stationary*, and of a star-like appearance: it is lighted throughout the night, and is seen at the distance of three or four leagues, or at lesser distances, according to the state of the atmosphere.

CORSEWALL LIGHT.

Situate on the Point of Corsewall, near the entrance to Loch Ryan, in Wigtonshire.

Corsewall Light *revolves*, exhibiting from the same light-room a light resembling a star of the first magnitude, and one of a brilliant red colour, the one after the other. Each light appears in its brightest state at intervals of every two minutes, and gradually becoming less luminous, is eclipsed. The light of the natural or star-like appearance is visible at the distance of about six leagues, and the red coloured light at four leagues, or at lesser distances when the state of the atmosphere is hazy or unfavourable.

AYR HARBOUR LIGHTS.

Situate upon the larboard hand in entering the harbour of Ayr, in Ayrshire. These three lights are *stationary*. Two of them are exhibited throughout the night from the same building, for the direction of vessels in the bay. The upper one has a star-like appearance, and may be seen at the distance of four leagues; but the other, which is tinged with red colour, is seen at not more than three leagues, or at lesser distances if the atmosphere be hazy. The third or tide-light, which is of a star-like appearance, is only exhibited while there are eight feet of water upon the bar; and being lower than the others, is not visible at so great a distance. When these three lights are seen in one line, they bear from one another S. E. by E. $\frac{1}{4}$ E., and N. W. by W. $\frac{1}{4}$ W., and are leading lights for entering the harbour.

TROON HARBOUR LIGHT.

Exhibited from the north gable-wall of a row of storehouses situate on the starboard hand in entering the Harbour of Troon in Ayrshire. This light, which is from gas, and is exhibited throughout the night, after being in its brightest state once in every minute, is suddenly eclipsed.

ARDROSSAN HARBOUR LIGHT.

SITUATE on the starboard hand in entering the harbour of Ardrossan in Ayrshire. This small light is exhibited throughout the night, and is visible at the distance of one or two miles, or at lesser distances when the atmosphere is unfavourable or hazy.

CUMBRAE LIGHT.

Erected upon the western side of the Little Cumbrae Island, in the County of Ayr, and Frith of Clyde.

THIS light is *stationary*, appearing like a star of the first magnitude, at the distance of three or four leagues, or at lesser distances in an unfavourable or hazy state of the atmosphere.

TOWARD LIGHT.

Situate in the Frith of Clyde, on the point of Toward, being the southern extremity of the district of Cowal in Argyleshire.

This light *revolves*, and is seen at the distance of two or three leagues, or at lesser distances when the atmosphere is hazy. The light appears once in every minute in its brightest state, having a star-like appearance, and gradually becoming less luminous, is eclipsed.

CLOUGH LIGHT.

Erected on the Clough Point, in the county of Renfrew, and Frith of Clyde, about 5 miles below the Port of Greenock.

This light is *stationary*, appearing like a star of the first magnitude, at the distance of three or four leagues, or at lesser distances when the weather is hazy.

NOTE.—*The Cumbrae, Toward, and Clough Lights are under the Cumbrae Light Trust, consisting of the Magistrates of Glasgow, Port-Glasgow, and Greenock. These Lights have lately undergone a complete repair, which has added much to their brilliancy and general effect.*

GREENOCK HARBOUR LIGHT.

Upon the Custom-house Pier of Greenock, in the county of Renfrew, a light of a star-like appearance is erected, as a direction generally for the harbour Lights of a red colour are also exhibited at the several entrances of this harbour.

PORT-GLASGOW HARBOUR LIGHT.

Upon the Pier of Port-Glasgow, in the county of Renfrew, a light of a star-like appearance is placed as a direction for the steamboats on the river, and for the Harbour of Port-Glasgow. The entrance to this harbour is also pointed out by a light of a red colour, placed on the West Quay.

BOWLING BAY HARBOUR LIGHT.

On the larboard side in going up the river Clyde, and starboard hand in entering the sea-lock of the Forth and Clyde Canal, at Bowling Bay, in Dumbartonshire, a small light, of a star-like appearance, is exhibited during the night.

GLASGOW OR BROOMIELAW QUAY LIGHT.

On the lower or western extremity of the Broomielaw Quay, and the larboard hand going up the river, a light of a star-like appearance is placed for the direction of the shipping.

PLADDA LIGHTS.

Erected upon the small Island of Pladda, situate in the Frith of Clyde, off the south-western point of Arran Island, in the county of Bute.

These lights are *stationary*, and erected upon separate towers, the one higher than the other. They appear like two stars of the first magnitude, at the distance of four or five leagues, or at lesser distances, according to the state of the atmosphere. When seen in one line, they bear from each other N. and S.

CAMPBELTON HARBOUR LIGHT.

Within Campbelton Loch in Argyleshire, a light of a star-like appearance is exhibited throughout the night, which, when brought to bear W. ½ N., leads into the Loch through the proper channel, on the northern side of the Island Devaar.

MULL OF KINTYRE LIGHT.

Erected on the south-western extremity of the Mull of Kintyre in Argyleshire.

This light is *stationary*, appearing like a star of the first magnitude, at the distance of six or seven leagues, or at lesser distances when the atmosphere is hazy.

RHINNS OF ISLAY LIGHT.

The Rhinns is the south-western headland of the Island of Islay, in the county of Argyle; and the Lighthouse is erected upon the small Island of Oversay, which is almost contiguous to the main island.

This light is known to mariners as a *flashing light*, which, in every twelve seconds, emerges from a state of partial darkness, and exhibits a momentary light, resembling a star of the first magnitude. It is visible at the distance of five or six leagues, or at lesser distances, according to the state of the atmosphere. The lantern is open toward Laggan Bay, within Loch-in-daal, and seaward between the headlands of Kinglyvie and Tanvore in Islay, or from N. N. E. to S. E. seaward.

LISMORE LIGHT.

The Commissioners of the Northern Lighthouses having resolved upon the erection of a lighthouse on the south-western extremity of the Island of Lismore in Argyleshire, the works commenced in the summer of 1830 ; *and when lighted, due notice will be given of its appearance. This light will form a direction to the Caledonian and Crinan Canals, and to the Sounds of Mull and Islay.*

BARA HEAD LIGHT.

The Commissioners of the Northern Lighthouses having also resolved on the erection of a lighthouse upon the Island of Berneray or Bara Head, forming the southern extremity of the Uist, Harris, and Lewis Isles, the works commenced in 1830, and due notice will be given of the appearance of the light, which will form a guide to the western entrance of the Minsh, or Frith of Uist, and for vessels on a foreign voyage making the land of the western coast.

ISLAND GLASS LIGHT.

Situate on the eastern side of Glass, one of the Harris Isles, in the county of Inverness, and on the western side of the channel between Skye and the Long Island.

This light is *stationary*, appearing like a star of the first magnitude at the distance of four or five leagues, or at lesser distances in hazy weather.

STORNOWAY HARBOUR, IN THE LEWIS ISLES.

A small light is proposed to be erected at Stornoway, which, when lighted, will be made known to the public.

CAPE WRATH LIGHT.

Situate on the headland of that name, in the county of Sutherland.

This light *revolves*, exhibiting from the same light-room two lights, the one resembling a star of the first magnitude, and the other being of a brilliant red colour. Each light appears in its brightest state, the one after the other, at intervals of two minutes, and gradually becoming less luminous, *is eclipsed*. The light of the natural or star-like appearance is visible at the distance of seven leagues, and the red light at five leagues, and intervening distances, according to the state of the atmosphere.

DUNNET HEAD LIGHT.

Situate on the northern extremity of Dunnet Head, in the county of Caithness.

This light will be exhibited in the course of the summer of 1831. It will be *stationary*, appearing like a star of the first magnitude at the distance of seven or eight leagues, or at lesser distances in hazy weather.

SUMBURGH HEAD LIGHT.

Erected upon Sumburgh Head, the most southern headland of the Shetland Islands.

This light is *stationary*, appearing like a star of the first magnitude, at the distance of seven or eight leagues, or at lesser distances in hazy weather. The lantern is open from Foula to Hang-cliff Head, in Noss Island, or from N. W. by N. ¼ N. to S. E. by E. ¼ E. southerly.

START POINT LIGHT.

Erected on the Island of Sanday, the most eastern point of land in Orkney.

This light *revolves*, and is seen at the distance of four or five leagues, or at lesser distances when the atmosphere is hazy. The light appears in its brightest state, like a star of the first magnitude, once in every minute, and gradually becoming less luminous, is eclipsed.

Note.—*Prior to the erection of the Start Point Lighthouse in the year* 1806, *a light was exhibited on the Island of North Ronaldsay, seven miles northward of the Start. North Ronaldsay Light was discontinued in* 1806, *agreeably to public notice, and the tower of masonry left as a Beacon.*

PENTLAND SKERRIES LIGHTS.

Placed on the larger of the Pentland Skerry Islands, at the eastern entrance of the Pentland Frith in Orkney.

These lights are *stationary*, erected upon separate towers, the one higher than the other, and appearing like two stars of the first magnitude, at the distance of four or five leagues, or at lesser distances in a hazy state of the atmosphere. When seen in one line with each other, they appear almost as one light, and bear from each other S.S.W. and N.N.E. In that position, they are leading lights for the foul ground to the southward of the Skerry.

Note.—*These lights are undergoing improvement, and as they are to be considerably elevated, and otherwise improved, they will appear more brilliant, and will be seen at a greater distance.*

TARBETNESS LIGHT.

Erected on the eastern extremity of Tarbetness, in Cromartyshire.

This light is known to mariners as an *Intermittent Light*. It suddenly appears like a star of the first magnitude, and continues in view 2½ minutes; it is then suddenly eclipsed for half a minute, and thus produces its entire effect once in every three minutes. It is visible at the distance of five or six leagues, and at lesser distances, according to the state of the atmosphere.

KINNAIRD HEAD LIGHT.

Situate in the county of Aberdeen, at the entrance to the Moray Frith, on Kinnaird Head.

This light is *stationary*, appearing like a star of the first magnitude, at the distance of five or six leagues, or at lesser distances in hazy weather.

BUCHANNESS LIGHT.

Placed on Buchanness, in the county of Aberdeen, the most eastern point of the main land of Scotland.

This light is known to mariners as a *flashing light*, which, in every five seconds of time, emerges from a state of partial darkness, and exhibits a momentary light, resembling a star of the first magnitude. It is visible at the distance of five or six leagues, or at lesser distances, according to the state of the atmosphere.

ABERDEEN HARBOUR LIGHT,

Situate on the northern pier-head or starboard hand in entering the harbour of Aberdeen, in the county of that name, is *stationary*. It is exhibited while there are nine feet of water on the bar.

Note.—It is proposed to improve this light. When altered, its appearance will be made known to the public.

GIRDLENESS.

The Commissioners of the Northern Lighthouses having resolved on the erection of a Lighthouse on Girdleness, in Kincardineshire, the works will commence in the summer of 1831; and due notice will be given of the exhibition of the light.

MONTROSE HARBOUR LIGHTS.

Situate on the starboard hand in entering the harbour of Montrose, in the county of Forfar. These two lights are *stationary*, and of a brilliant red colour. One of them is higher than the other, and when seen in one line, they bear from each other N.W. by W. ¾ W., and S.E. by E. ¾ E., and are leading lights for the Annet Sand-bank.

ARBROATH HARBOUR LIGHT.

A small *stationary* light, of a red colour, is placed on the northern pier-head and starboard hand in entering the harbour of Arbroath in Forfarshire. It is lighted by the pilots only when ships appearing in the bay have water into the harbour. The light is seen at the distance of two or three miles, or at lesser distances when the atmosphere is hazy.

BELL ROCK LIGHT.

The Sunk Rock on which this Light is erected, is exposed to view at low water of spring tides, and is situate off the Friths of Forth and Tay, 11 miles S. by E. ⅓ E. from Arbroath, in the county of Forfar.

This Light *revolves*, exhibiting from the same light-room a light resembling, in its brightest state, a star of the first magnitude, and one of a brilliant red colour, the one after the other. Each of these lights appears at intervals of two minutes, and gradually becoming less luminous, is eclipsed. The light of the natural or star-like appearance is seen at the distance of five leagues, and the red coloured light at four leagues, or at lesser distances when the atmosphere is hazy. During foggy weather and snow-showers, a bell is tolled at intervals of half a minute.

NOTE.—*For a description of this arduous undertaking, see " Stevenson's Account of the Bell Rock Lighthouse."*

BUTTONNESS LIGHTS.

Situate on the northern side of the entrance to the Frith of Tay, in the county of Forfar.

THESE two lights are *stationary*, erected upon separate towers, the one higher than the other, and appearing like stars of the first magnitude at the distance of three or four leagues, or at lesser distances in hazy weather When seen in one line, they bear from each other N. N.W. ½ W., and S.S.E. ½ E., and are leading lights for the Gaa and Abertay Sands, at the entrance of the Tay.

SOUTH FERRY NESS LIGHS.

Situate in the county of Fife, within the Frith of Tay, and on the southern side.

These lights are *stationary*, erected upon separate towers, the one somewhat higher than the other, and have a star-like appearance at the distance of one or two leagues, or at lesser distances in a hazy state of the atmosphere. When seen in one line, they bear from each other N.W. by W. ⅝ W., and S.E. by E. ⅝ E., and are a leading direction for the fair-way, in clearing the Abertay Sands.

DUNDEE HARBOUR LIGHTS.

A light of a red colour is erected on the East Pier, and on the starboard hand at the entrance of Dundee Harbour, in Forfarshire; and another on the Middle Pier, on the larboard hand in entering the Wet Docks, having a star-like appearance. These lights are of the same height, and bear from each other S.E. $\frac{3}{4}$ E., and N.W. $\frac{3}{4}$ W. When seen in one line, they are leading lights for clearing the southern side of the Beacon Rock. They are visible at the distance of one or two leagues, or at lesser distances in a hazy state of the atmosphere.

DUNDEE FERRY LIGHTS.

At the Craig Pier of Dundee, on the Forfar side of the Frith of Tay, a *stationary* light is exhibited throughout the night for the direction of the ferry boats.

At Newport, on the Fife side of the ferry,

two lights are erected, the one somewhat higher than the other, which bear S.S.W. and N.N.E. from each other, and are leading lights for clearing the east end of the Middle Bank.

ISLE OF MAY LIGHT.

Erected upon the Isle of May, situate in the Frith of Forth, and county of Fife.

This Light is *stationary*, appearing like a star of the first magnitude, at the distance of six or seven leagues, or at lesser distances when the atmosphere is hazy.

CARR ROCK BEACON.

The Carr Rock Beacon is erected upon the outer or seaward of the Carr Rocks. It consists of a circular basement of masonry, on which is placed a spur-beacon of cast-iron, terminating in a ball formed with ribs of iron, measuring 3 feet 6 inches in diameter, and elevated 30 feet above low water-mark.

INCHKEITH LIGHT.

Erected on the Island of Inchkeith, situate in the Frith of Forth, and county of Fife.

This light *revolves*, and is seen at the distance of four or five leagues, or at lesser distances, according to the state of the atmosphere. It appears in its brightest state like a star of the first magnitude, once in every minute; and gradually becoming less luminous, is eclipsed.

LEITH HARBOUR LIGHT.

Erected upon the pier-head, on the larboard hand in entering the harbour of Leith, in the county of Mid-Lothian. This light is *stationary*, and is exhibited while there are 9 feet of water on the bar. It is seen at the distance of one or two leagues, or at lesser distances, in a hazy state of the atmosphere. In the daytime a train of signals is used in relation to the rise of the tide, commencing with one ball at the top of the flag-staff when there are 9 feet water on the bar.

Note.—A temporary lantern, from which a light of a red colour is exhibited, is placed at the end of the extended pier.

NEWHAVEN HARBOUR LIGHT.

A SMALL *stationary* light of a red colour is lighted upon the pier at Newhaven, in the county of Mid-Lothian; but is only exhibited when the passage-boats ply in the night. It may be seen at the distance of two or three miles, or at lesser distances in a hazy state of the atmosphere.

KINGHORN HARBOUR LIGHT.

A SMALL *stationary* light of a star-like appearance is exhibited on the starboard hand in entering the harbour of Kinghorn, in the county of Fife, while there are 8 feet of water in the harbour. It may be seen at the distance of two or three leagues, or at lesser distances when the atmosphere is hazy.

BURNTISLAND HARBOUR LIGHT.

A SMALL *stationary* light is exhibited throughout the night, on the starboard hand in entering the harbour of Burntisland, in the county of Fife. It is seen at the distance of two or three leagues, or at lesser distances in a hazy state of the atmosphere.

QUEENSFERRY LIGHTS.

A *stationary* light is exhibited at the principal ferry slips or piers at North Queensferry, in the county of Fife, and another at Newhalls, near South Queensferry, in the county of Linlithgow, which are lighted for the use of the ferry-boats throughout the night, excepting in clear moon-light.

NOTE.

The Public Lights on the coast of Scotland, and Isle of Man, and the Floating Buoys in the Frith of Forth, are under the direction of the Commissioners of the Northern Lighthouses.

LIGHTS

ON THE

IRISH COAST.

LIGHTS

ON THE

IRISH COAST.

DUBLIN HARBOUR LIGHT.

Is placed on the eastern extremity of the Pier of Dublin, and larboard hand in entering the harbour. This light is *stationary*, and is lighted throughout the night. There is also a signal light from half flood to half ebb; and during the same period of the tide in the day, a flag is hoisted. The light is seen at the distance of two or three leagues, or at lesser distances when the atmosphere is hazy.

KINGSTOWN HARBOUR LIGHT

Is erected on the Eastern Pier, and larboard hand in entering the Harbour of Dunleary, now Kingstown, in the county of Dublin, and on the southern side of the bay. This light *revolves*, is lighted throughout the night, and is seen at the distance of two or three leagues, or at lesser distances in a hazy state of the atmosphere.

HOWTH BAYLEY LIGHT.

Situate on the northern side of the entrance to the Bay of Dublin, in the county of that name.

This light is *stationary*, appearing like a star of the first magnitude at the distance of four or five leagues, or at lesser distances in a hazy state of the atmosphere.

HOWTH HARBOUR LIGHT.

Erected on the Eastern Pier-head of Howth Harbour, in the county of Dublin. This light is *stationary*, and exhibits a brilliant red colour throughout the night.

KISH BANK FLOATING-LIGHT VESSEL.

Moored in 8 Fathoms Water, at the Northern end of Kish Bank, about 3 Leagues S.E. from Dublin Harbour Light.

The Kish Float exhibits three lights from separate masts, which, from the main-mast being the highest, have a triangular figure. These lights appear *steady*, or *in motion*, according to the state of the weather, and are seen at the distance of two or three leagues, or at lesser distances when the atmosphere is hazy. In the day a flag is hoisted at the mast-head; and during foggy weather and snow showers, a bell is tolled night and day.

WICKLOW HEAD LIGHTS.

Situate on Wicklow Head, the eastern extremity of the county of Wicklow.

THESE lights are *stationary*, erected upon separate towers, the one higher than the other, and appear like two stars of the first magnitude, at the distance of five or six leagues, or at lesser distances, according to the state of the atmosphere. When seen in one line, they bear from each other N.W. by W. ¾ W., and S.E. by E. ¾ E., and are leading lights between the India and Arklow Banks.

ARKLOW BANK FLOATING-LIGHT VESSEL.

Moored within the southern side of Arklow Bank, in 16 Fathoms Water, bearing from Wicklow Head Lights S.S.W., distant 13 Miles; and from the Tusker Light N.E. by N. ¼ E. distant 33 Miles.

ARKLOW BANK FLOAT exhibits one light, which appears *steady*, or *in motion*, according to the state of the weather. It is visible at the distance of two or three leagues, or at lesser distances in hazy weather. In the day a flag is hoisted at the mast-head; and during foggy weather and snow showers, a bell is tolled night and day.

TUSKER LIGHT.

The Rock on which this Light is erected is situate off the county of Wexford, about 9 Miles E.S.E. ¼ E. from Carnsore Point, the south-eastern extremity of the mainland of Ireland.

This light *revolves*, exhibiting from the same light-room two lights, like stars of the first magnitude, the one after the other, and then a light of a brilliant red colour; each of these three lights appearing at intervals of two minutes. After being at their brightest state, they gradually become less luminous, and are eclipsed. The lights of the natural or starlike appearance are visible at the distance of five leagues, and the red light at four leagues, or at lesser distances in a hazy state of the atmosphere. During foggy weather and snow showers, a bell is tolled night and day at intervals of half a minute.

SALTEES CONINGBEG FLOATING-LIGHT VESSEL.

Moored in 20 *Fathoms Water, off the Coast of Wexford, bearing S.W. ¼ W., about* 3 *Miles from the Great Saltee Island, and bearing W. from Tusker Light, distant* 20 *Miles.*

The Saltees Float exhibits two lights from separate masts, the one higher than the other, which appear *steady,* or *in motion,* according to the state of the weather. These lights are visible at the distance of two or three leagues, or at lesser distances, when the weather is hazy. In the day a flag is hoisted at the masthead; and during foggy weather and snow showers, a bell is tolled night and day.

HOOK TOWER LIGHT.

Situate on the eastern side of the entrance to Waterford Harbour, in the county of Wexford.

This light is *stationary*, appearing like a star of the first magnitude, at the distance of four or five leagues, or at lesser distances when the atmosphere is hazy.

DUNMORE HARBOUR LIGHT.

The harbour of Dunmore lies about a mile S.W. of Creyden Head, on the larboard side entering Waterford, in the county of that name. The light is placed at the extremity of the pier, on the south side of the harbour's mouth: it is a light of two faces, the one to the sea, of a deep red colour, and visible some time before passing the Hook Tower Light; the other face looking to the harbour is a clear bright light, but is not visible on coming down the river before being a-breast of Creyden Head.

DUNCANNON LIGHTS.

Situate at the Fort of that name, in the county of Wexford, within the river, on the eastern or starboard side, in going up to Waterford.

These lights are *stationary*, and erected on the same tower, the one above the other. They appear like stars of the first magnitude, at the distance of three or four leagues, or at lesser distances according to the state of the atmosphere. When seen in one line with each other, they form leading lights between Bluff Head and Dunmore Sand Banks.

CORK LIGHT.

Situate on the northern side of the entrance to Cork Harbour, in the county of Cork.

This light is *stationary*, and is of a brilliant red colour seaward, which is seen at the distance of three or four leagues, or at lesser distances in a hazy state of the atmosphere. Landward, the light is of the natural appearance.

KINSALE HARBOUR LIGHT.

PLACED on Fort Charles, on the eastern side of Kinsale Harbour, in the county of Cork. It is *stationary*, and appears like a star of the first magnitude, at the distance of three or four leagues, or at lesser distances when the atmosphere is hazy.

OLD HEAD OF KINSALE LIGHT.

Erected on the Old Head of Kinsale, about 5 Miles S. W. by S. of the Harbour of Kinsale, in the county of Cork.

THIS light is *stationary*, appearing like a star of the first magnitude, at the distance of four or five leagues, or at lesser distances in a hazy state of the atmosphere.

CAPE CLEAR LIGHT.

Cape Clear Island, on which this Light is erected, is the most southern land of Ireland, and lies off the mainland of the county of Cork.

This light *revolves*, and is seen at the distance of six or seven leagues, or at lesser distances in a hazy state of the atmosphere. The light appears once in every two minutes in its brightest state, like a star of the first magnitude, and gradually becoming less luminous, is eclipsed.

SKELLIGS ROCK LIGHTS.

Erected on the Skelligs Rocks, situate off Bolus Head, in the county of Kerry, from which they bear W.N.W. and are distant 3 Leagues; and from Brae Head, in the Island of Valentia, they bear S.W. ¼ W., and are distant 8 Miles.

These lights are *stationary*, erected upon separate towers, the one higher than the other, and appear like two stars of the first magnitude, at the distance of four or five leagues, or at lesser distances when the atmosphere is hazy. When seen in one line, they bear from each other N. by E. and S. by W., and form a direction for the Foze and Bull Rocks, by keeping the two lights about a handspoke open from each other.

LOOPHEAD LIGHT.

Situate on Loophead, on the northern side of the River Shannon, in the county of Clare.

This light is *stationary*, appearing like a star of the first magnitude, at the distance of five or six leagues, or at lesser distances in hazy weather.

KILKADRAAN HEAD LIGHT.

Situate on the northern side of the Shannon, about 12 miles E. from Loophead, in the county of Clare.

This light is *stationary*, and is of a brilliant red colour seaward, which is seen at the distance of three or four leagues, or at lesser distances in a hazy state of the atmosphere. Landward, the light is of the natural appearance.

SOUTH ARRAN LIGHT.

South Arran Island, on which this Lighthouse is erected, is situate off the Mainland of the county of Clare, at the entrance of Galway Bay.

This light *revolves*, and is seen at the distance of five or six leagues, or at lesser distances in hazy weather. The light appears once in every three minutes in its brightest state, like a star of the first magnitude, and gradually becoming less luminous, is eclipsed.

GALWAY HARBOUR LIGHT.

ERECTED on Mutton Island, situate on the western side of the entrance to Galway Road and Harbour, in the county of Galway. This light is *stationary*, and is of a brilliant red colour seaward, which is seen at the distance of three or four leagues, or at lesser distances when the atmosphere is hazy. Landward, the light is of the natural appearance.

SLINE HEAD LIGHT.

THE Commissioners of the Ballast-Office, Dublin, have resolved upon the erection of a Lighthouse upon Sline Head, an island lying off the coast of the county of Galway. When lighted, due notice will be given of its appearance.

CLARE ISLAND LIGHT.

Erected on the north-eastern point of Clare Island, situate on the entrance of Clew Bay, and in the county of Mayo.

This light is *stationary*, appearing like a star of the first magnitude, at the distance of five or six leagues, or at lesser distances in a hazy state of the atmosphere.

WESTPORT AND NEWPORT HARBOUR LIGHT.

Erected on the Island of Innis Gurth, situate about four miles from Westport, and the same distance from Newport, in the county of Mayo. This light is *stationary*, having a star-like appearance at the distance of two or three leagues, or at lesser distances in a hazy state of the atmosphere. This light is useful among the numerous small islands of Clew Bay, and as a guide to Westport and Newport Harbours.

EAGLE ISLAND LIGHT.

The Commissioners of the Ballast-Office, Dublin, have resolved upon the erection of a Lighthouse upon Eagle Island, off the coast of the county of Mayo. When lighted, due notice will be given of its appearance.

KILLYBEGS LIGHT.

The Commissioners of the Ballast Office, Dublin, have resolved upon the erection of a Lighthouse upon St John's Cape, in the county of Donnegal, on the northern side of Donnegal Bay. It is intended to be a stationary *light, and will appear like a star of the first magnitude.*

ARRAN MORE, OR NORTH ARRAN LIGHT.

Erected on the northern side of North Arran Island, situate off the Mainland, county of Donnegal.

THIS light is *stationary*, appearing like a star of the first magnitude, at the distance of four or five leagues, or at lesser distances when the atmosphere is hazy.

NOTE.—*On the exhibition of the proposed Light on Tory Island, Arran More Light will be discontinued.*

TORY ISLAND LIGHT.

THE Commissioners of the Ballast Office, Dublin, have resolved upon the erection of a Lighthouse upon Tory Island, lying off the coast of Donnegal. It is proposed to be a stationary *light, and will appear like a star of the first magnitude.*

LOUGHSWILLY LIGHT.

Erected on Fannet Point, situate on the western side of the entrance to Loughswilly, in the county of Donnegal.

THIS light is *stationary*, and is of a brilliant red colour seaward, which is seen at the distance of three or four leagues, or at lesser distances in a hazy state of the atmosphere. Towards the Lough, the light is of the natural appearance.

INNISTRAHULL LIGHT.

Erected on the Island of Innistrahull, situate off the Mainland, in a central position between the Loughs Swilly and Foyle, in the county of Donnegal.

THIS light *revolves*, and is seen at the distance of six or seven leagues, or at lesser distances when the weather is hazy. The light appears once in every two minutes, in its brightest state, like a star of the first magnitude; and gradually becoming less luminous, is eclipsed.

MAIDEN OR HULIN ROCKS LIGHTS.

Situate off the north-eastern coast of the county of Antrim.

These lights are *stationary*, and will be seen like two stars of the first magnitude, at the distance of four or five leagues, or at lesser distances in a hazy state of the atmosphere. The lights are erected upon rocks 320 fathoms apart, which bear from each other N.W. by W. and S.E. by E., but the foul grounds of the Maidens extend about one league to the southward of the rocks on which the lights are erected.

COPELAND LIGHT.

Erected on Cross Island, lying half a mile N.E. from the Island of Copeland, off the coast of Down county, and on the south-eastern side of Belfast Lough.

This light is *stationary*, appearing like a star of the first magnitude at the distance of five or six leagues, or at lesser distances, when the atmosphere is hazy.

DONAGHADEE HARBOUR LIGHT.

Situate on the larboard hand in entering the harbour of Donaghadee, in the county of Down. This light is *stationary*, and is of a starlike appearance. It is lighted throughout the night, and is visible at the distance of two or three leagues, or at lesser distances in a hazy state of the atmosphere.

SOUTH ROCK LIGHT.

The sunken Rock on which this Light is erected is situate off the mainland of Downshire, about two leagues northward from the entrance to Lough Strangford.

This light *revolves*, and is seen at the distance of three or four leagues, or at lesser distances in a hazy state of the atmosphere. The light appears once in every minute in its brightest state, like a star of the first magnitude, and gradually becoming less luminous is eclipsed.

ARDGLASS HARBOUR LIGHT.

Erected on the pier head, on the larboard hand in entering the harbour of Ardglass, in the county of Down, about 3 miles south-westward from Lough Strangford. This light is *stationary*, and is of a brilliant red colour seaward, which is seen at the distance of two or three leagues, or at lesser distances when the atmosphere is hazy.

CARLINGFORD LIGHTS.

This Lighthouse is erected on Halbowling Rock, situate within Lough Carlingford, about the middle of the Channel leading to Newry, in the county of Down.

These two lights are *stationary*, and are placed on the same tower, the one above the other. The higher light is exhibited throughout the night, and will be seen like a star of the first magnitude at the distance of four or five leagues, or at lesser distances if the atmosphere is hazy. The lower light, having also a starlike appearance, is exhibited from half-tide to half-tide. In the day, during the same period of tide, a ball is hoisted upon a pole; and during foggy weather and snow-showers a bell is tolled night and day, at intervals of half a minute.

CARLINGFORD LOUGH LIGHT.

This Lighthouse is situate on Greenore Point, upon the larboard side in going up Carlingford Lough, in the county of Louth.

THIS light is on the revolving principle, and of the natural appearance, and attains its greatest magnitude once in every fifteen seconds.

BALBRIGGAN HARBOUR LIGHT.

ERECTED on the larboard hand in entering the harbour of Balbriggan, situate in the county of Dublin, about 9 miles south from Drogheda. This light is *stationary*, and is of a brilliant red colour seaward, which is seen at the distance of two or three leagues, or at lesser distances in a hazy state of the atmosphere. Landward, the light is of the natural appearance.

NOTE.

The Public Lights on the Coast of Ireland, are under the direction of The Commissioners of the Ballast-Office, Dublin.

FINIS.

PRINTED BY NEILL & CO.
Old Fishmarket, Edinburgh.

This book should be returned to the Library on or before the last date stamped below.

A fine of five cents a day is incurred by retaining it beyond the specified time.

Please return promptly.

NOV 13 1924

FEB 16 1931

Milton Keynes UK
Ingram Content Group UK Ltd.
UKHW022253271123
433389UK00005B/242